A Gallery of Reflections:

the Nativity of Christ

A Gallery

The Nativity of Christ

RICHARD HARRIES

# of Reflections

WILLIAM B. EERDMANS PUBLISHING COMPANY
GRAND RAPIDS, MICHIGAN

Text © 1995 Richard Harries

First published 1995 in the U.K. by
Lion Publishing, Oxford

This edition published 1996
through special arrangement with Lion by
Wm. B. Eerdmans Publishing Co.
255 Jefferson Ave. S.E., Grand Rapids, Michigan 49503

Printed in Spain

ISBN 0-8028-3814-6

Contents

Interest in the arts has never been greater. As a result of television and the opportunities provided to travel and visit the great art galleries of the world, millions of people love the visual arts. For many, this love of the arts—the visual arts as well as music—has a spiritual dimension. Art can sustain, inspire and give solace, particularly in a time when the candle of faith in society as a whole has burnt low.

Towards the end of 1992 the National Gallery kindly invited me to do their 'Picture of the Month', which they publish in their monthly news sheet. I selected the picture by Geertgen which appears in this collection. This opportunity made me see the possibility of doing a whole series of reflections focused upon one particular theme in art and the result is this *Gallery of Reflections*. It does two things.

First, it tries to set a particular painting in its historical context. Art history is a fascinating subject and, as a result of the popularizing work by people like the late Sir Kenneth Clark, many enjoy seeing the unfolding of a particular period. Secondly, there is a spiritual side to this. The majority of the great artists in European history have not only been part of a culture that has been ostensibly religious, they themselves have been people of faith—sometimes profound, troubled or passionate faith. Each artist has had a particular feel for life, an individual way of seeing things, a unique understanding of the birth of Christ and its importance. So that in entering into the outlook of the artist we can enter more deeply into some aspect of the truth of God incarnate.

There are many books on art history and there are a few books of spiritual reflection on particular pictures. *A Gallery of Reflections* tries to bring these two approaches together. To do this is, I believe, neither illegitimate nor forced, because for the vast majority of artists, painting a religious scene was itself a religious act. They did not think of religious pictures simply as cultural adornments or status symbols. These were expressions of faith and devotion. The art expressed the faith, and the faith flowed into shapes and colours and arrangements.

This book also seeks to see the tradition of Christian painting on the Nativity as a whole. From the Renaissance until our own times, it was fashionable to disparage icons and Byzantine work generally as Greek and primitive. Partly as a result of modern movements in art we have rediscovered the importance of a more symbolic religious art—indeed sometimes it seems the only way in which religion can be expressed in art. From the other side—the side of the Orthodox Church—the achievements of the Renaissance, however technically brilliant, have seemed degenerate, a departure from the spiritual norm. Certainly one sometimes feels the truth of this and it remains a great puzzle. We can still sense something of the numinous, the awe-inspiring, in the paintings of the early Renaissance from Sienna, and in Giotto. By the time we come to Raphael and even Michelangelo, however much we admire their superb works, they don't on the whole prompt us to kneel. Was something essential lost at the Renaissance, or is every generation's understanding of what is and what is not numinous culturally conditioned? Although I am much drawn by icons and Byzantine work generally, I do not take the view that Western religious art has no spiritual depth. The spirituality inherent in it is expressed in different ways, as I try to show in the reflections on different paintings.

When I first began this study, there seemed a dearth of twentieth-century paintings on the Nativity. There is no shortage of religious art, including good religious art, in our own time. But for understandable reasons the cross of Christ has been central. However, Canon Keith Walker and The Revd Tom Devonshire-Jones alerted me to some paintings that I might otherwise have

ICON OF THE NATIVITY Cyprus, sixteenth century

overlooked, and to them both I am extremely grateful. Inevitably I have only been able to reflect on a tiny percentage of the vast number of Nativity scenes in every age, including our own. This is only a very small collection but it does, I hope, represent something of the range, depth and riches of Christian art on this theme.

The Nativity story traditionally takes us from the Annunciation through to the Presentation of Christ in the Temple and that order has been followed in this book. However, there is a particular focus on the Nativity itself, in particular the worship of the kings and shepherds.

Christian depiction of the Nativity begins in the catacombs and is now expressed in the art of almost every culture in the world. If space had allowed, there would have been more scenes chosen from the Christian art of, for example, India, China and Africa. The focus here is European with just a reminder that there is much good Christian art in other cultures.

Personally I find this kind of study of great interest and I hope it will be of interest to many others who love the visual arts. I hope it might also prove helpful to those who find spiritual sustenance and solace through the arts. For those whose thoughts topple over into meditation and whose yearnings are at least sometimes expressed in prayer, I hope that the pictures in this book, and the reflections, will provide an aid to meditation and prayer of all kinds.

Richard Oxon:
OXFORD, 1995

The earliest Christian art

ART IN THE CATACOMBS— The Epitaph of Severa

Underneath the streets and houses of Rome lie the catacombs. It was in these vast underground burial chambers that the first Christians lay their dead in expectation of the resurrection. Much of the walls of the catacombs are covered with simple drawings and frescos. It is here that we have our first visual evidence of how they saw the faith. In the catacomb of Priscilla, there is a painting of the Adoration of the Magi on an arch which dates from the second century. It depicts the Virgin Mary seated with the Christ child on her lap and the three Magi approaching to do homage. In that same catacomb of Priscilla there was found a moving epitaph of a woman called Severa. The inscription wishes her a life in God and her clothing signifies that she was of the nobility. This epitaph also depicts the three Magi coming to adore the Christ child. Joseph stands behind Mary's seat pointing at her, the divine star hangs above and the three kings come dancing along, with their Phrygian caps and cloaks flying out at the back making them look for all the world like graceful dragonflies.

This scene of the Adoration of the Magi was the first and most widely used Christian symbol for the Nativity, therefore for the whole sweep of human redemption through Christ. The noble Roman lady by having this sign on her epitaph indicates that she too wishes to do homage to the Christ child.

The scene of the three Magi also appears on sarcophagi from the fourth century onwards, on the walls of other catacombs and in the fourth-century mosaics of the Church of Santa Maria Maggiore in Rome. The picture of kings bringing homage was the way in which Romans depicted the submission of a conquered city. The monument of Theodosius I in Istanbul, for example, depicts the emperor watching the chariot races and, below him, conquered kings kneeling with their gifts. It was natural that Christians should take over this imperial iconography. The three Magi, already beginning to take on some of the characteristics of kings, show the pomp and power of the world kneeling in homage before the Christ child, the King of kings.

Although the picture of the three kings approaching the seated Virgin was the most usual way of depicting the Nativity, other details familiar to us also appear in some representations. The lid of this fourth-century sarcophagus, for example, shows not only the Magi approaching and the star, but the animals, Christ in the manger, Joseph standing and Mary sitting.

AN EARLY CHRISTIAN AMPULLA

When Helena, the mother of the Emperor Constantine, discovered the places associated with the life of Christ in the fourth century, the Holy Land gradually became a place of pilgrimage. Like all pilgrims, those early Christian spiritual travellers wished to take back souvenirs. A number of them have survived. They are small flasks, ampullae, and, very often, Christian scenes are depicted on them. One from the sixth century, originally from Palestine shows another depiction of the Nativity which owes much to imperial imagery. The emperors had themselves depicted in regal splendour, sitting on the throne with their subjects doing obeisance. In this portrayal of the Nativity, the Virgin Mary is depicted as an empress, with the star above her—the star which for the pagan world depicted the divine presence—and the three kings on one side and the shepherds on the other, symmetrically balanced.

During the two centuries and more in which the iconoclastic controversy raged, most Christian art of the time was destroyed. Since then there have been endless further destructions, particularly when the Venetians burnt and sacked Constantinople in 1204. So it is not surprising that little of the art of this earlier period survives. What did sometimes survive were ivories, and some exquisite icons in ivory can be found in the world's major museums. For although we associate the word 'icon' with religious paintings on wood, the word simply means 'image', and Christians were quite happy to use any material—tapestry, metal or ivory—to keep before them the picture of God incarnate, his mother and the saints.

One familiar scene, throughout Christian history, is Mary seated in majesty on a throne, with the Christ child on her lap. Another is the icon of the Nativity which will be discussed on page 30. But clearly there was a period of transition from the early pictures, in the catacombs and on sarcophagi, of kings bringing their presents to the Christ child, with Mary present, to the fully developed iconography of the Nativity with which we are familiar. This icon on ivory shows one stage of the transition. The unarticulated, tubular bodies and inexpressive faces, the draperies described by shallow parallel lines are thought to resemble seventh- to eighth-century Palestinian icons. In the top half Mary sits in majesty with the child Jesus on her lap, whilst the kings bring presents on one side, supported by worshipping angels on the other.

In the lower panel Mary lies on her pallet whilst Joseph beside her points to a star. Jesus lies on a crib which has come to resemble an altar, his life being one of sacrifice. On either side the ass and the ox, very prominent, turn towards the Christ child in worship. Below the Christ child a woman named Salome stands, her hand withered when she doubts the virgin birth, one of the incidents related in the *Protoevangelium of James*.

So the lower panel depicts details and incidents associated with the birth. But the upper, larger panel directs us to the object of our worship, the Christ himself. Mary holds Christ in her lap, setting him before the viewer for adoration.

*I*n the sixth month the angel Gabriel was sent by God to a town in Galilee called Nazareth, to a virgin engaged to a man whose name was Joseph, of the house of David. The virgin's name was Mary. And he came to her and said, 'Greetings, favoured one! The Lord is with you.' But she was much perplexed by his words and pondered what sort of greeting this might be. The angel said to her, 'Do not be afraid, Mary, for you have found favour with God. And now, you will conceive in your womb and bear a son, and you will name him Jesus. He will be great, and will be called the Son of the Most High, and the Lord God will give to him the throne of his ancestor David. He will reign over the house of Jacob forever, and of his kingdom there will be no end.' Mary said to the angel, 'How can this be, since I am a virgin?' The angel said to her, 'The Holy Spirit will come upon you, and the power of the Most High will overshadow you; therefore the child to be born will be holy; he will be called Son of God. And now, your relative Elizabeth in her old age has also conceived a son; and this is the sixth month for her who was said to be barren. For nothing will be impossible with God.' Then Mary said, 'Here am I, the servant of the Lord; let it be with me according to your word.' Then the angel departed from her.

LUKE 1:26–38

From the sixth century the feast of the Annunciation has been kept on 25 March. However in some places before then, the festival was celebrated on the first or second Sunday before Christmas as part of the Nativity celebrations. So, understandably, we still read this story at Christmas time and associate it with the birth of Christ. For he is no ordinary child. The angel Gabriel appeared to his mother, Mary and she was overshadowed by the Holy Spirit.

First depicted in the third century, this lovely scene soon appeared everywhere, on jewellery, doors, illustrating St Luke's Gospel and on icons. Mary was shown standing or sitting on a throne. In a fifth-century mosaic on the triumphal arch of the Church of Santa Maria Maggiore in Rome, Gabriel is shown flying overhead. From this date a well and purple wool were often shown, details from the *Protoevangelium of James*, a book of stories about the birth and infancy of Christ dating from the middle of the second century.

Once the great iconoclastic controversy was over (the dispute about whether or not there should be a Christian representative art) in the ninth century, many beautiful features associated with this scene appeared—spring-time elements, flowers and a closed garden. From earlier than this and right through to our own time Gabriel is usually shown carrying a lily, a sign of purity. The lily as the sign of purity was taken over from ancient Greece, where it was said to have sprung from the milk of Hera, the wife of Zeus.

In order to indicate that Jesus was miraculously conceived, from the sixth century the Annunciation scene showed a ray of light and a dove coming down from heaven. From the ninth century the same affirmation was made in a more startling manner. A child was shown in Mary's breast, sometimes in a circle or mandorla (pointed oval). One of these can be seen, for example, in a famous twelfth-century icon of the Annunciation from St Catherine's Monastery at Sinai and also in an icon in the Tretyakov Gallery in Moscow. This scene is clearly related to the icon known as the 'Virgin of the Sign' or *Blachernitissa*, in which Mary is shown with both hands upwards, praying (the *orans* position), and the infant Jesus in a circle is shown at her breast facing the onlooker.

Later versions show Mary reading or at prayer with the angel poised or kneeling before her. It was a scene loved and painted by all the great artists of the Renaissance.

THE ANNUNCIATION by Fra Angelico

I love the icons of the Orthodox Church and believe they are able to point beyond themselves to God in a way that most religious paintings do not. For all their technical skill and beauty, many Renaissance paintings seem to lack this sense of the transcendent or numinous—the sense of the awe-inspiring presence of God.

However, I would certainly make one exception. When it comes to scenes of the Annunciation I prefer Renaissance treatments to those of the Orthodox Church. Here, remarkably, Renaissance skill and subtlety are combined with a pre-Renaissance feel for spiritual things. This is especially true of Fra Angelico (1387–1455).

In 1432 Fra Angelico painted an Annunciation scene for a church in Cortona. It depicts Mary and the angel inside a beautiful Renaissance loggia (an open-sided arcade) of the type designed by the architect Filippo Brunelleschi. The angel is richly attired in red and gold, and Mary too is dressed in bright colours. In the picture depicted here, however, which he painted about 1440, all this gold and jewellery and colour was abandoned in favour of a composition of the utmost simplicity. Instead of the loggia of the earlier painting, with its garden, and doorway leading into another room, it depicts a cell-like chamber closed by a blind wall, which had the double function of providing a background for the figures and of discouraging the mind from straying from the confines of the scene. It is characteristic of a tendency to eliminate extraneous detail that even the capitals of the two columns are covered by the angel's wings.

It has been pointed out that the Renaissance architect Alberti distinguished between beauty and ornament, the former deriving from a system of harmonious proportion, the latter consisting of the columns and other decorative features of a building. It would seem there is some such distinction in Fra Angelico's mind here, as in his other frescos in the monastery, for he avoids anything ornamental. On the other hand, the vaulting that has been painted on the back wall—like an abstract pattern, yet one indicating depth—has all the beauty of harmonious proportion.

The nineteenth-century art historian Ruskin remarked that 'Angelico is not an artist properly so-called but an inspired saint'. We know what he means, for his paintings have a profound spirituality. But the remark is thoroughly misleading. Angelico was a trained artist, fully in touch with the latest developments of the time. No less important, his religion was not a personal, private affair but a corporate one. He was a monk, a member of the Dominican Order, which discouraged individual inspiration and sought to maintain the tradition of art in the service of religion. The famous frescos which he and his assistants painted for the restored convent buildings of San Marco were at once the expression of, and a guide to, the spiritual life, and the discipline and devotion of the community. In each cell he painted a fresco to inspire and guide its occupant. The fresco shown here is from cell 3. Lucky monk, we feel, who was allowed to live there.

In this picture there is a sense of the 'timeless moment'. All is stillness and mystery and gentleness. We need no elaborative details. The clear lines, subdued colouring and the look going back and forwards from the angel to Mary say it all. We hardly need the words, 'Hail, Mary, full of grace . . .' 'Behold the handmaid of the Lord; be it unto me according to thy word' to know what is going on. It is all in the look.

*I*n those days Mary set out and went with haste to a Judean town in the hill country, where she entered the house of Zechariah and greeted Elizabeth. When Elizabeth heard Mary's greeting, the child leaped in her womb. And Elizabeth was filled with the Holy Spirit and exclaimed with a loud cry, 'Blessed are you among women, and blessed is the fruit of your womb. And why has this happened to me, that the mother of my Lord comes to me? For as soon as I heard the sound of your greeting, the child in my womb leaped for joy. And blessed is she who believed that there would be a fulfilment of what was spoken to her by the Lord.'

And Mary said,
'My soul magnifies the Lord,
and my spirit rejoices in God my Saviour,
for he has looked with favour on the lowliness of his servant.
Surely, from now on all generations will call me blessed;
for the Mighty One has done great things for me,
and holy is his name.
His mercy is for those who fear him
from generation to generation.
He has shown strength with his arm;
he has scattered the proud in the thoughts of their hearts.
He has brought down the powerful from their thrones,
and lifted up the lowly;
he has filled the hungry with good things,
and sent the rich away empty.
He has helped his servant Israel,
in remembrance of his mercy,
according to the promise he made to our ancestors,
to Abraham and to his descendants forever.'

And Mary remained with her about three months and then returned to her home.

LUKE 1:39–56

THE VISITATION by Rueland Frueauf the Elder

In Christian art the embrace of a husband and wife has sometimes been depicted in order to symbolize the special nature of the birth of their child. For example, Giotto painted the embrace of Mary's parents, Joachim and Anna, in order to convey the idea that her conception was immaculate, that she was conceived without sin. So such embraces in Christian art are not only a warm human encounter but they have theological meaning. Similarly, the scene of Mary and Elizabeth embracing is also a symbolic pointer to the special nature of the birth of Jesus. Certainly, in early Christian art, this scene—which we usually call the Visitation but which in the Orthodox Church is called the Embrace or *Aspasmos*—appears with the scene of the Annunciation.

Rueland Frueauf the Elder (c. 1445–1507) was a native of Salzburg who worked in the Passau region. His late Gothic art was characterized by expressive figures and affectionately represented landscapes. It is the figures which impress us in this lovely depiction of the Visitation.

Our eyes are drawn first to the face of Elizabeth on the right. It is a face at once strong and gentle, wise and feminine, patient, human and holy. It looks as if it is the face of a nun, one who bears within herself some of the suffering of the world, who in later life would become a much revered and loved Mother Superior. But she is Elizabeth, pregnant with John the Baptist, greeting Mary, pregnant with the Christ child. Both women look down in awe before the mystery of pregnancy and birth; in awe before the mystery of God's providence in their lives.

Above all in this picture our eyes are drawn to their hands. Each holds the other's hand or arms in a twofold embrace, one which is both gentle and firm. It suggests mutual feeling, comfort and support.

For me this holding of hands and arms has a universal appeal because it speaks of the way women have supported other women in every age. In a world so often dominated by cruel men, a world in which women have been oppressed or marginalized, women have so often clung together and supported one another through all eventualities. Above all has this been true in times of pregnancy and birth. This is a scene from which men are excluded, not deliberately or malevolently, but because two women are meeting and supporting one another in face of the great mystery of life of which they supremely are aware.

THE VISITATION by Gloria Guevara

In 1966 a Nicaraguan priest, Ernesto Cardenal, began a small Christian commune amongst some poor farmers and fisher folk in Solentiname. The peasants in that area began to understand the gospel in a new way, as liberation not only for themselves but for their oppressed society. In 1977 the National Guard destroyed most of the peasants' huts and the church was turned into a military barracks. However, in 1979 the oppressive régime was itself overthrown and the peasants returned to rebuild Solentiname. The reflections of the peasants in that commune on the gospel were collected and published and some of them were later republished in *The Gospel in Art by the Peasants of Solentiname*, together with pictures related to those reflections.

One of the reflections in relation to this picture is from a woman called Andrea who says about Mary's *Magnificat*, 'She recognizes liberation... We have to do the same thing.

Liberation is from sin, that is, from selfishness, from injustice, from misery—from everything that's oppressive. That liberation is in our wombs too, it seems to me...' Another man, called William, remarked, 'But the people can't be liberated by others. They must liberate themselves. God can show the way to the Promised Land, but the people themselves must begin the journey.' In this picture the Promised Land, in idealized form, can be seen through the opening at the rear of the hut, a kind of paradise on earth. Within the hut Elizabeth, greying and in spectacles, worn down by life yet still vigorous, kneels before Mary. Mary stands, a strong figure, her feet firmly on the ground, her jaw four-square, facing life with determination. Here is a woman whom God has liberated and through whom God will liberate others, enabling them to take responsibility for their own destiny and the destiny of the society in which they are set.

*I*n those days a decree went out from Emperor Augustus that all the world should be registered. This was the first registration and was taken while Quirinius was governor of Syria. All went to their own towns to be registered. Joseph also went from the town of Nazareth in Galilee to Judea, to the city of David called Bethlehem, because he was descended from the house and family of David. He went to be registered with Mary, to whom he was engaged and who was expecting a child. While they were there, the time came for her to deliver her child. And she gave birth to her firstborn son and wrapped him in bands of cloth, and laid him in a manger, because there was no place for them in the inn.

LUKE 2:1–7

This is a classic icon of the Nativity from Russia by a follower of Andrei Rubliev, the great fouteenth-century painter. Details of this icon are discussed in the following pages. Here we look at the icon as a whole.

Although this icon contains a number of different scenes, it does not come across like a cartoon with one event following another or each event isolated. On the contrary, there is a wonderful harmony about the icon centred on the Christ child.

Two invisible horizontal lines run across the icon. Below Mary we have scenes from the earth. Around Mary, in the middle section we have the union of heaven and earth, with the earth worshipping that divine union in Christ. Above the cave we have the worship of heaven, with the rays from the star shining down upon the infant child.

In the bottom section we have the joys and sorrows of life, the natural happiness of the two midwives washing the Christ child on the right-hand side and, on the left, a depressed, tempted Joseph. In the middle section both the great ones and the little ones come to worship the Christ child, both kings and shepherds. But worship is not confined to humanity alone. On the contrary, the animal creation takes its place, the ox and ass bow over the crib. And around the icon trees blossom and flourish on the rocky mountain. The whole of creation is affected. Then, in the upper section, the angels sing their unceasing praise, one of them bowing low before the child.

All revolves around the babe in the crib in the dark cave. Starting from the right-hand side, the angel bows low, the shepherd looks heavenward, the women pour their water, Joseph just sits, the angels bow in reverence and the kings make their journey. Here we see the unity and joy of the whole created order as it is centred upon the Word made flesh. All things, even the melancholic Joseph, take their place in the dance.

In a traditional icon we see the truth of the incarnation of God proclaimed—that God has become a human being. But we also see the effect of that incarnation upon the whole creation. In the words of St Gregory the theologian, the Nativity of Christ is 'a festival of re-creation'. For Christ came to consecrate and renew the whole universe. As Vladimir Lossky puts it, 'through the incarnation of God, the whole of creation acquires a new meaning, lying in the final purpose of its being—its ultimate transfiguration'.

We, too, are invited to take our place, to centre our day upon Christ who is the beginning of the transfiguration (or transformation) of all creation and its goal. The service of Vespers in the Christmas liturgy of the Orthodox Church puts it this way:

What shall we bring thee, O Christ, when thou art born on earth as man for our sakes; for each of the creatures, who have their being from thee, bring thanks to thee: angels their songs, the heavens a star, the wise men gifts, the shepherds wonder, the earth a cave, the wilderness a manger, but we—the Virgin Mother.

We could add that the icon also shows gifts from the animal and vegetable world. We too can hear the music and join in the dance, and bring the gift of ourselves before the humble God.

In traditional icons—that is, icons as they had developed by the fourteenth century in Russia and which have set the iconography since then—Mary seems to dominate the scene. For eyes used to Renaissance pictures, in which Mary is shown presenting the child, before whom others kneel, it is somewhat startling that in the icon she is so large, spread-eagled across the picture and in a pose whose spiritual meaning is not obvious.

Mary is lying on a pallet, the kind of bed that Jews carried when they travelled. It is the bed on which she gave birth to the Christ child. Her face is meditative but her body rests after her labour. Quite simply, she is exhausted.

And at times in the history of the church it has been important to stress this, for it highlights the fact that Jesus was truly born, the incarnation is real. He did not come on earth as a ghost or phantom. He came from the womb of Mary, and Mary went through all the labour of childbirth. Mary's tiredness is a sign that God has indeed become a human being.

The other reason that she is so central is that she is the first-born of the new creation. The early Fathers liked to say that God became man in order that man might become divine. We also are to share in God's life. Mary is the first to whom the benefits of the incarnation apply; she is 'the renewal of all born on earth'. For as Eve became the mother of all living people, so the new Eve becomes the mother of all renewed humanity which is deified through the incarnation of the Son of God. So the pallet on which she sleeps is a royal red, acting as a kind of mandorla against which the new humanity is outlined.

The Son of God was truly born; he was born that we might be reborn with the new life of God he came to bring us. We rejoice in him not only for his sake, but for our own.

THE TEMPTATION OF JOSEPH

In this traditional icon, in the bottom left-hand corner there is a dark figure, huddled up and withdrawn into himself. Beside him is an old man in a rough coat holding a stick. This is the temptation of Joseph.

We do not learn much about Joseph in the New Testament. Luke, however, emphasizes his presence with Mary, and Matthew recalls a series of dreams that Joseph had, especially the one that told him not to be afraid of marrying Mary, for her child was not that of another man but of God himself, and she remained a virgin. Inevitably, though, the Christian imagination got to work on Joseph at an early stage and various stories became associated with him. In art he first appears in images of the Nativity on some fifth-century ivories. After that he retained his peripheral but abiding place on the Nativity scene.

Joseph is not part of the central group of the child and Mary, for he is not the father and is emphatically separated from this group. Before him, in the disguise of an old bent shepherd, stands the devil, tempting him. On some icons this old man is represented with small horns or a short tail. Certain early texts speak of the doubts of Joseph and his troubled state of mind. So he appears pressed and withdrawn. The devil tempts Joseph by telling him that the virgin birth is not possible, being opposed to the laws of nature—an argument which has reappeared in every period of human history.

Despite the ancient iconography, the predicament of Joseph is a very modern one. For who would not be put out to find that the woman to whom he was engaged was pregnant in a mysterious manner? Who would not be put out to know that he was not the father of the child? Who would not be put out to know that he would have to play second fiddle, or indeed third fiddle, to the Christ child and Mary, the virgin mother. Thoroughly left out, Joseph sinks into a mood of

self-pity, doubt and resentment. As if that were not enough, there is the ancient doubt about whether this birth is indeed the result of a miraculous conception as the Gospels proclaim. As we know, it is in such black moods that temptation comes and we do not need an old man in front of us, let alone one with horns and a tail, to remind us that temptation is all too real. Some icons depict dogs which seem ill at ease, snapping and restless.

When such darkness takes hold of us, it's no good cheerful souls telling us to snap out of it, or assuring us that things are not as bad as we think. The fact is, that's how we feel.

One of the helpful features of this scene is that we do not see Joseph having snapped out of it, all bright and beaming. His dejection is simply recognized for what it is. Even in our most depressed moments and blackest moods we have a place before God incarnate, within the circle of love. We can be there, as we are. God in Christ is with us, however little we are able to take in the fact. We are given permission to be there, before the Christ child, even if it means simply sitting full of doubt and sadness.

On this traditional icon of the Nativity, in addition to the familiar characters, there is an unusual scene at the bottom right-hand corner. Two young women are shown bathing a baby.

There is no mention of this scene in the Gospels. However, in the document known to us as the *Protoevangelium of James*, dating from the second century, much is made of the role of midwives. The function of the midwife is also made quite clear, even if that function is by our standards in bad taste. It is to witness that Mary is still *virgo intacta*.

In the icon as we have received it, however, the midwives are not there giving evidence. They are simply washing the new-born babe. It is quite clear that this imagery was taken over more or less whole from pagan depictions of the birth of gods and great men. We have a similar scene for example in Paphos, Cyprus, depicting the birth of Dionysus, and another in Beirut showing the birth of Alexander the Great. When Christianity became the established religion of the Roman Empire, it took over royal imagery. It was as natural to associate the birth of Jesus with this scene as it is for us to associate royalty with a crown.

So the scene has had different meanings at different times.

Whilst we should value our rich heritage of literature and art, we should also be encouraged to use our creative imagination in interpreting what is before us, without being tied to previous meanings (and we may not always be sure of these). The presence of those two women at the birth of Jesus is highly significant for us today. First, the preciousness of every child: our culture is sickened with stories of children being abused or, in their turn, being violent to others. Yet every child begins as a little Christ, a miracle. If our society is to get out of its present awful mess we need to devote all the resources we can, and more, to babies and children. We need to maximize what we spend on pre-school provision of every kind.

Secondly, Mary was not alone. While she lies on her pallet exhausted, the two young women care for the babe. It's no good simply lamenting the breakdown of the traditional family hoping it will one day come back. We need to take all the steps we can now to support mothers (and fathers) of all kinds. In Oxford for example we have not only 'Parentline', but 'Homestart' and a family nurturing programme. This helps people to come to terms with the way they themselves have been nurtured in order that they may be better able to nurture their own offspring. Children and parents are helped together, and come to enjoy one another more.

These two young girls beside Mary, gently holding the Christ child, suggest to me that wider community who today have such a vital role in nurturing and supporting parents and their young children—children who are Christ in embryo.

THE CAVE, AND THE CHRIST CHILD

In the centre of the icon is a dark hole, a black cave. The Gospels say nothing about a cave. The tradition that Jesus was born in one dates from the second century and it has persisted since then, so if you go to Bethlehem today you will be shown a cave under the Church of the Nativity. In the icon, however, the cave is more than a place where Christ was born. Its blackness symbolizes human ignorance and sin, our absorption with ourselves, and our neglect or ill treatment of others.

Into our darkness came the Word incarnate—God become human. The Christ child is wrapped in swaddling clothes, bringing to mind the shrouds in which his dead body was wrapped. The cave itself foreshadows the tomb in which he was laid. In some icons the crib takes the form of a stone altar, indicating the sacrifice of Christ, through his life, death and burial for our redemption.

In this darkness the ox and the ass loom, bending their heads over the crib (because the ass was not known in Russia, in some Russian icons a horse is depicted with an ox).

God loves us and brings us up as his children but so often we turn away from the light and turn our backs on the love which beckons us. Yet all is not lost. Although we human beings rebel, nature in its own way offers praise to God. I think of a rainbow and its meaning in the story of Noah. Human wickedness is such that we cannot think why God goes on tolerating human life; we wonder why he does not simply wipe it all out and start again. But the rainbow is a reminder that God's mercy remains and that however bad things are, nature will continue to sustain us; seed time and harvest time will not fail. Here the ox and the ass, in their own way, acknowledge the Lord of creation.

Every tree and plant and animal and bird praises God just by being. A line of the poet W.H. Auden suggests that birds chirp, not for effect, but because that is the thing to do. In doing their thing, they praise God. What is our thing? The glory of human beings is that we are called to offer conscious praise. Although we rebel, that is still our vocation and destiny. Through union with the incarnate Word, in love and prayer, we can join the ox and ass in offering the praise of our lives.

Scenes of the Nativity almost invariably show an ox and ass by the crib. There is no mention of these animals in the New Testament story so why did they appear? They made their entry via a verse in the book of Isaiah (1:3).

The ox knows its owner,
and the donkey its master's crib;
but Israel does not know,
my people do not understand.

This verse was referred to by commentators from the second century onwards and it seems clearly to be in the mind of Luke even though he does not specifically refer to it. Three times he refers to the crib and in doing this he obviously has some special purpose. This purpose is to bring out the fact that the message of this verse in Isaiah has been repealed; for Israel, through the shepherds, has begun to know, has begun to understand. The shepherds are a sign that some, at least, of God's own people are coming to faith in Jesus.

The animals appear in Christian art from at least the fourth century onwards, as has been seen on the sarcophagus on page 14 and they appear in nearly all the Nativity scenes in this book. They are prominent in the scene from the thirteenth-century Winchester Bible (opposite).

The crib scene began to be especially popular after Francis of Assisi had a crib at the midnight mass in 1223 and his love of poverty has influenced interpretation of it ever since—Christ born poor amongst the poor.

The animals however have had different meanings in different ages. For Luke, as I have said, the fact that Jesus was born in a crib was a sign that the people of God would now believe. However, it was not long before the presence of the ox and ass at that crib became a silent reproach to Jews who would not acknowledge Jesus as the Messiah. The clear implication was that the ox and ass were prepared to share in the joy of the incarnation whereas Israel still was not willing to know or understand. Later the presence of these two animals were taken to be a sign of God's care for the Christ child. In Ludolf of Saxony's *Vita Christi* the writer claimed to have seen the Nativity and described how 'the ox and the ass, kneeling down, put their mouths to the crib, breathing through their noses on to the Child, because they knew that at that cold time he needed to be heated up in that manner'. This expression of care is present in the Chartres jube, pictured below, where Joseph is shown putting a blanket over Mary and the ox and ass are at either end of the crib in a solicitous manner.

Subsequent reflection sometimes drew a distinction between the ox, patient and sacrificial, and the ass, less willing to kneel and sometimes a symbol of lewdness. But for us, they are a sign that the whole of creation shares in the joy of Christ's Nativity. We are part of the whole animal creation and every aspect offers praise to God in its own way, by being itself.

In the *Benedicite*, which begins, 'O all ye works of the Lord, bless ye the Lord', the whole of creation praises God, including the animals.

'O all ye beasts and cattle, bless ye the Lord: praise him and magnify him for ever.' The ox and ass take their place there. The next verse of the *Benedicite* reads, 'O ye children of men, bless ye the Lord: praise him and magnify him for ever.' We too are called to join in the great hymn of praise to God our creator who has shown us his heart of love in his Son.

Whenever I hear the song of the angels in Luke's Gospel read, it brings to mind the wonderful music of Handel's *Messiah*:

And suddenly there was with the angel a multitude of the heavenly host praising God and saying, 'Glory to God in the highest, and peace on earth, good will toward men.'

According to Jewish tradition the angels sang when God created the earth. We know that in the temple the prophet Isaiah had a vision of the angels praising God. At the new creation brought about by the birth of Christ, once again heaven and earth are caught up in an ecstasy of praise. For here also is the climax of creation, with all things glorifying God and divine peace coming from God to embrace and bless his people.

Yasuo Ueno is a Japanese artist, born in 1926 and currently a professor at Tamma Art College in Tokyo. As a child he once lost a gift he had been given at a Sunday school party. But the teacher found the gift and came next day to give it to young Yasuo. He writes:

Even now after so many years, that gift, a book of Bible pictures, is one of my treasures. For many years I have wanted to paint the Christmas story. Once begun, I thought of that Christmas Day—of myself and my teacher, and his care and concern for this unhappy child, and his replacing the lost book. Now more than thirty years later, if I could somehow present my book, The First Christmas, to him, I would indeed be grateful.

In this picture from his Christmas book we seem to have a window into another world. The unusual combination of colours both on the outside and within the frame indicate that we are being taken into another dimension. Who knows what angels look like? Normally they are depicted with features, looking like particularly beautiful human beings. But Yasuo Ueno has wisely left their faces indistinct. What they convey is a sense of lightness, of joy, of motes dancing in the sunlight.

The poet Francis Thompson once wrote that:

The angels keep their ancient places;—
Turn but a stone, and start a wing!
'Tis ye, 'tis your estrangèd faces,
That miss the many-splendoured thing.
'THE KINGDOM OF GOD'

If we could see as God sees, all would shimmer with glory, all would be taken up in the divine dance. Most of us do not have this experience. But it is part of the mind of Christ, the mind of the church, which we can begin to make our own as we join with the angels and one another to say:

Glory to God in the highest,
and peace to his people on earth.

Hosios Lucas is a lovely monastery about an hour's drive from Delphi, north of the Bay of Corinth in Greece. The Luke it commemorates is not the Gospel-writer, but a local, holy monk. The monastery has some wonderful mosaics. Dating from 1011, they are a little earlier, though better preserved, than the mosaics in the better-known monastery of Daphni near Athens.

In Orthodox churches, all heaven is depicted. Christ the creator and judge is in the dome surrounded by angels and archangels with, perhaps, the prophets. In the squinches—the architectural structures which enable a dome to be built over a square building—there appear the four main Gospel scenes, one of which was the Nativity. This squinch is half conical, so there is a slight element of crowding in the scene.

All the main elements of Orthodox iconography are present: Christ in his crib in the centre, with the ox and the ass looking down; then, moving to the right of the picture as we look at it, the midwives bathing the infant Christ, and the shepherds. On the other side there is Joseph looking pensively at the child and behind are three kings, two tiny and one enormous. However, the picture is dominated by the angels. To the right there are two angels, one of them looking down on the shepherds and blessing them with the revelation of the Christ. The other one is bending down pointing to the Christ child

in the crib. On the other side of the mosaic three angels with prominent wings bend forward, two looking down at Christ, one towards the kings.

The angels are very much part of the world of the Nativity. They take their place with the shepherds and the animals and the kings. Indeed in this mosaic they are more prominent than any other participant with the exception of Mary and the Christ child. People at this time had a strong sense of heaven being close to us; hence the whole company of heaven being present at, and rejoicing in, the incarnation. Heaven and earth seem part of one, unified world.

We do not know what to make of angels. Are they simply a picturesque way of talking about the divine? Or do they represent individual realities of another order? Answering these questions is less important than having a sense of that other world interfused with the one we daily inhabit.

The birth of Jesus was not the arrival of a lonely child in a lonely family on a lonely planet. It was surrounded by the delight of the whole company of heaven. In this mosaic, a great ray comes from heaven shining through the sky, pointing to the Christ child. This birth *is* special. But so is every birth. Christ came in order that we might become what he eternally is. The angels surround us and rejoice in us too.

The church in which this fresco appears is one of a number of remarkable small churches in the Troodos mountains in central Cyprus. Because of their location, they remained isolated and relatively free from the ravages of occupying powers. So the wonderful paintings which cover the walls remain well preserved. The name derives from *arakas* (pea), like so many of the appellations of the Virgin Mary in Cyprus deriving from plants and vegetables. This Nativity scene like others in the nave was completed by 1192. Byzantine art at its best combines a number of different approaches. It has a Christian iconography, in which the painting points beyond itself to spiritual truth. But the Byzantines, who spoke Greek, also looked back to classical Greek civilization and its art with its beautiful forms. It also looked back to the Hellenistic period, when human characteristics and features were strongly displayed in that art. Just after this church was completed, in 1204, Constantinople was destroyed by the Fourth Crusade. Before that date Constantinople was the centre of an artistic enterprise and style that went all over the Byzantine world. It was a style that brought together the classical, the natural and Christian symbolism in a satisfying whole. This style is most wonderfully preserved in this Nativity scene. Here the metropolitan, classicizing school is in its full bloom, the climax of Byzantine art of the middle period (ninth to twelfth centuries).

There are one or two unusual details of this picture worth noting.

Joseph, instead of being tempted by a shepherd/devil figure, is consoling himself by talking to a donkey. On the other hand the animals behind the crib seem to have disappeared. The crib itself, as in some earlier depictions, is in the form of an altar, for the Christ child is born for a life and death of sacrifice. On the bottom right-hand side two sheep are standing still. This reflects a remarkable passage in the *Protoevangelium of James*. As Joseph went out to look for a midwife, he experienced a mystical moment in which the world stood still.

And I Joseph was walking, and was not walking; and I looked up into the sky, and saw the sky astonished; and I looked up to the pole of the heavens, and saw it standing, and the birds of the air keeping still. And I looked down upon the earth, and saw a trough lying, and work people were climbing: and their hands were in the trough. And those that were eating did not eat, and those that were rising did not carry it up, and those that were conveying anything to their mouths did not convey it; but the faces of all were looking upwards. And I saw the sheep walking, and the shepherd raised his hand to strike them, and his hand remained up. And I looked upon the current of the river, and I saw the mouths of the kids resting on the water and not drinking, and all things in a moment were driven from their course.

The picture is, however, dominated by Mary on a white—as opposed to the usual red—mattress. And above her the angels stream in to do homage to the Christ child. The fresco as a whole is both striking and satisfying. The various incidents blend together in a harmonious whole. In particular the colours, yellow and brown and white, have a warmth and freshness about them. This is the kind of picture about which we instinctively want to say at a first look, 'How beautiful.' This sense of its beauty is enhanced by looking at the details. The midwife bathing Christ, for example, is far from the ugly midwife of earlier depictions. She is a beautiful girl who would certainly feel at home in a court. In the top right-hand corner one of the young shepherds is as handsome as any youth that appeared in ancient Greece. Mary's face is sweet and soulful.

Above her the angels have classical good looks and their wings and garments have all the elegance and style one could possibly want. In short, the Nativity is here depicted in a way which seeks to be aesthetically pleasing in every aspect. Christ is able to redeem what strikes us as broken and ugly. Indeed it is the distinctive contribution of Christianity that nothing is outside the reach of God's redemptive action.

Nevertheless, Christianity is not only interested in the dark side of life. All that is healthy and harmonious, free and flowing, rejoices God's heart. The beautiful lines of classical Greek art can be baptized in Christ, so can the humanism of the Hellenistic period. All that is elegant and pleasing, all that is harmonious and delightful, classical good looks and all that is beautiful—all this is baptized in Christ. All this takes its place round the Christ child, rejoicing in the wonder of God's creation and his re-creation of us in Christ.

*I*n the time of King Herod, after Jesus was born in Bethlehem of Judea, wise men from the East came to Jerusalem, asking, 'Where is the child who has been born king of the Jews? For we observed his star at its rising, and have come to pay him homage.' When King Herod heard this, he was frightened, and all Jerusalem with him; and calling together all the chief priests and scribes of the people, he inquired of them where the Messiah was to be born. They told him, 'In Bethlehem of Judea; for so it has been written by the prophet:

"And you, Bethlehem, in the land of Judah,
are by no means least among the rulers of Judah;
for from you shall come a ruler
who is to shepherd my people Israel."'

Then Herod secretly called for the wise men and learned from them the exact time when the star had appeared. Then he sent them to Bethlehem, saying, 'Go and search diligently for the child; and when you have found him, bring me word so that I may also go and pay him homage.' When they had heard the king, they set out; and there, ahead of them, went the star that they had seen at its rising, until it stopped over the place where the child was. When they saw that the star had stopped, they were overwhelmed with joy. On entering the house, they saw the child with Mary his mother; and they knelt down and paid him homage. Then, opening their treasure chests, they offered him gifts of gold, frankincense, and myrrh.

MATTHEW 2:1–11

46

From at least the fifth century, Christians began to decorate scriptural texts with small illustrations. In due course the custom grew up of turning the initial letter of a book or chapter into a picture. There are many gorgeous initial letters in the illuminated manuscripts of the Middle Ages. Eric Gill (1882–1940) helped to revive this craft. He began by earning his living as a letter-cutter but became well-known as a sculptor, engraver and writer—as well as a typographer. In 1913 he became a Roman Catholic and was commissioned to make the *Stations of the Cross* at Westminster Cathedral which, together with his *Prospero and Ariel* on the outside of Broadcasting House in London, are his best-known sculptures. He founded a religious guild of craftsmen with the object of promoting a revival of a religious attitude to art and craftsmanship.

All Gill's work, like this lettering and illustration, is characterized by clear, bold outlines and linear elegance. Here our eyes are drawn to the three kings with their hands upraised and we follow their figures down the flowing lines of their bodies and the folds of their garments. They are not kneeling but, as it were, saying, 'Hail, king of the Jews.' They could be figures from a ballet.

Mary, similarly, is in a graceful posture as she kneels, whilst the Christ child is presented naked and unashamed. He is held forth without covering or adornment for all to see. The great diagonal of the 'N' across the picture seems to give added emphasis to the 'NOW' of the birth of Jesus.

There seem to be no hidden depths in this illustration. All is expressed in the line and the movement; all, we might say, is incarnate—made flesh in what is visible and tangible.

The letters are of a piece with the picture in their boldness, style and elegance; letters and illustration form a unity.

Gill brought before the Christ child all the grace and elegance and style of which he was capable. There is a balletic beauty in the gestures and movement. It is a refreshing contrast to the hurried, scruffy, graceless way in which we live so much of our lives. If we are capable of any grace of body or mind, elegance of movement or life, beauty of design or art, this too is a gift worthy to bring and which is graciously received.

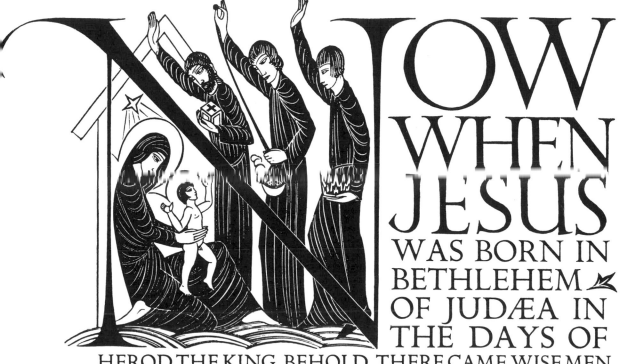

OW
WHEN
JESUS
WAS BORN IN
BETHLEHEM
OF JUDÆA IN
THE DAYS OF
HEROD THE KING, BEHOLD, THERE CAME WISE MEN
FROM THE EAST TO JERUSALEM, SAYING, WHERE IS
he that is born King of the Jews? for we have seen his star in
the east, & are come to worship him.

The mosaics in the churches of Ravenna are some of the most wonderful works of art in the world. The Church of St Apollinare Nuovo is a long, basilica-type building. All down one wall are tall figures of martyrs. All down the other are stately, gorgeously robed virgins. This mosaic of *The Three Kings* comes on the same side as the virgins, at the head of their column, bringing their gifts to the Christ child seated on the lap of an enthroned Mary, with two angels on either side. These superb mosaics date from the early part of the sixth century.

Green is a fashionable colour today. So it was then, helping to indicate paradise. The bright, luscious green of this mosaic contrasts well with the red and white. We take palm trees for granted as part of the scenery in the Middle East. But they are more than that. They appear not only in mosaics, but on elegantly carved sarcophogi of the fifth and sixth centuries, as images of eternity, a return to the paradise of Eden. Similarly, flowers are signs of that paradise. All around the feet of the kings, delightful flowers spring up. Dates hang from the branches of the palms. All is fruitful, bountiful, blessed.

The kings themselves are truly remarkable figures. On their heads are Phrygian caps. Phrygia was a region in Turkey and the Wise Men were sometimes thought to have come from there.

Even more arresting than the caps, however, is the stance of the three. They lean forwards, with their feet springing off the ground, all eagerness. Even at this early stage in the development of the tradition, one is depicted as old, with a white beard, one as middle-aged, with a dark beard, and one as young, without a beard at all. But they are all united in their hurry to come to the Christ child and offer their gifts. Their eyes and faces are focused forward, looking neither to the right nor to the left. The old one in the front appears to be almost running, whilst the cloak of the one in the rear is beginning to flow behind.

With what single-mindedness, with what eagerness, with what springing delight they bound forward to bring their gifts to the Christ child. Oh, if only we had a similar springing eagerness in the offering of ourselves.

In Padua, in the north of Italy, there is a chapel completely covered by Giotto frescos. This Scrovegni Chapel, named after the donor, tells the story of the birth and life of Christ in a series of panel pictures. Giotto (1266–1337) is one of those watershed names in art history; he more than any other is the one in whom the Renaissance in art is said to have begun. Art historians since Vasari in the fifteenth century have thought of him as humanizing what they saw as the wooden, stereotyped art of the Byzantine world. Certainly there are plenty of signs of humanity in this Nativity scene. Our eyes are drawn first of all to the two camel heads and the face of the retainer looking up. Most art, like most history, tends to concentrate on the big names, but most of us are part of the crowd. Giotto depicts one of the crowd, one of the king's retainers, not looking at the Christ child but up at the head of the camel. That camel seems to be drawn by Mary and the child—and perhaps, in due course, the retainer, following the gaze of the camel, will be drawn too. But for the moment, like most of us most of the time, he is distracted. Yet perhaps even now he is wondering what it is that has caught the attention of the camel.

Although art historians right through until the nineteenth century saw in Giotto and his successors a great advance on the art of the Byzantine world, something, I believe, was lost. Byzantine art points to the numinous, the divine, in a way that paintings of the late Renaissance, however technically superb, signally fail to do. Yet in Giotto that sense of the divine is still there.

I love Giotto not simply because of the human element but because the iconic quality of previous art—the capacity to point beyond itself to God—has not yet been lost: indeed it is still very much present.

Giotto in this scene has avoided a boring over-obvious symmetry by not placing the Christ child in the centre. Rather, the focus is shaped like a great 'V'-shape. One side of the 'V' is formed by the head of the camel, the two heads of the standing kings and the head of the kneeling king. The other longer side of the 'V' runs up from the head of the kneeling king through the Christ child and Mary to the top of the mountain—a mountain which is very reminiscent of mountains in icons. The tip of the 'V' is formed by the head of the kneeling king kissing the Christ child. If our eyes are caught at first by the head of the camel they are drawn down in reverence to that kneeling king. There is in this scene a sense of genuine devotion, reverence, piety and gentleness. One of the standing kings seems almost to be shying away with a sense of the unutterable humility of God becoming man. It is this atmosphere of tender reverence, which is at the very heart of the religious spirit, which makes this—as so many of Giotto's paintings—so special. Because our capacity for awe, reverence, even respect is so diminished in the modern world, we need Giotto to remind us what genuine devotion before the Holy One of God is like. Yet, in all of us, something of that capacity for tender reverence is still alive.

Our eyes are drawn by the wonderful colours. The shades of the yellows, browns, oranges and reds of the hats are warm and rich. They are matched by the transluscent whites, yellows and browns of the faces and bald pates of the Magi in the foreground. These colours are not brassy or vulgar. On the contrary they exude richness in every sense, sophistication and maturity. They are the colours of autumn—the world in its ripe maturity bringing its gifts to the Christ child.

Mantegna (1431–1506) in his early years painted in Padua and his sculptural style may have been influenced by Donatello who was active there in the 1440s. Mantegna loved to recreate the classical world in all its detail. In this scene we do not have the classical world, but the blue porcelain vessel carried by one of the Magi and the jasper and agate vessels carried by the other two were probably copied from the large collection of such ornaments in the possession of one of Mantegna's patrons.

This picture, painted between about 1497 and 1500 is wonderfully audacious. We are drawn right close into the scene. Instead of seeing the three kings from afar kneeling in the distance we are right in with them. The window through which we look cuts through the old Magus' beard, Joseph's head and the heads of the others. We are almost jammed in with them. This brings us face to face with the people depicted. The nearness is almost startling, accentuated as it is by Mantegna's clear line. The faces of the old Magus and the central one are not those of innocence. They are of people who know the world, people who have had positions of responsibility in it, people who have had to struggle and make hard decisions, people who have developed a range of sophisticated skills. Yet, together with this, they have retained a certain directness which they bring to bear from their hearts through their eyes to the Christ child.

Our closeness to Christ reveals us as we are. But Christ wants the real person, not a pretence or fraud. We are to come as we are, with all our experience of the world, lessons hard-won, skills acquired: with, Jesus said, the wisdom of serpents and the gentleness of doves.

Christians have used any available material to depict the objects of faith. Tapestry was a favourite material for early Egyptian Christians and some fine ones still survive from the fifth and sixth centuries. It was much loved by the medieval world and made a comeback with other things medieval during the nineteenth century. It suits the medieval, dream-like quality of this Nativity by Edward Burne-Jones.

Mary is set in a bower of flowers. Who has not sometimes had feelings of paradise walking in a rose garden? In both Islamic and Christian art flowers evoke a sense of what life could be and should be, perfected and beautiful. Mary especially is associated with flowers and in particular with the lily, which can be seen in this scene together with a range of other varieties.

The figures seem like characters from a medieval tale, Joseph gathering wood like a peasant woodcutter, one of the Wise Men dressed as a chivalrous knight in armour and Mary herself like a fairy princess at the bottom of her garden sitting in a rustic gazebo.

Yet the medieval world was not, of course, like this. What Burne-Jones gives us is the nineteenth-century Romantic view of that period. This was the one that depicted an ideal world of beautiful, chaste princesses, chivalrous knights who fell in love with them, honest woodcutters, all seen against a background of the supernatural world, including fairies and giants as well as angels. In this picture that supernatural world is evoked most powerfully by the forest in the background and its unearthly blue light. You feel that if you walked in that forest you would be at once thrilled and slightly scared.

Medieval romances and fairy tales are not as popular now as they were in the nineteenth century. Nevertheless, many human beings have at one time or another been touched by the romantic re-creation of that world. We know that it is an unreal world, the creation of the human imagination, yet something about it can still occasionally touch and haunt us. It is supernatural rather than religious; but supernatural in a way which is hospitable to a religious view of life. There is a still beauty about this scene, as though the Wise Men wandering in the woods have come across Mary in her bower of flowers and simply stopped in silent reverence, particularly well-depicted in the bowed head and look of the eyes of the first Wise Man.

Edward Burne-Jones (1833–98) was originally going to be ordained, but his interest turned to art at Oxford as a result of the influence of William Morris and in particular Dante Gabriel Rossetti. His dreamlike paintings have been regarded as a reaction to industrialization or as an escape from a world which he could not face. Neither explanation is the whole truth. That dreamlike world is part of all of us, nor is it simply the product of our unconscious. It is an ideal, a romance, a fantasy—but one which haunts us because it beckons us into the beautiful world which ours is meant to be and which, in God, it can become. Burne-Jones' tapestry is not the Nativity as it was, nor is it the Nativity as understood by people in the medieval period. It is a nineteenth-century Romantic view of the Nativity depicted in idealized medieval terms. It suggests to us that Jesus is the still centre of all worlds—Romantic, legendary, supernatural. There is no world, whether in the mind or outside it, of which he is not Lord.

In that region there were shepherds living in the fields, keeping watch over their flock by night. Then an angel of the Lord stood before them, and the glory of the Lord shone around them, and they were terrified. But the angel said to them, 'Do not be afraid; for see—I am bringing you good news of great joy for all the people: to you is born this day in the city of David a Saviour, who is the Messiah, the Lord. This will be a sign for you: you will find a child wrapped in bands of cloth and lying in a manger.' And suddenly there was with the angel a multitude of the heavenly host, praising God and saying,

'Glory to God in the highest heaven,
and on earth peace among those whom he favours!'

When the angels had left them and gone into heaven, the shepherds said to one another, 'Let us go now to Bethlehem and see this thing that has taken place, which the Lord has made known to us.' So they went with haste and found Mary and Joseph, and the child lying in the manger. When they saw this, they made known what had been told them about this child; and all who heard it were amazed at what the shepherds told them. But Mary treasured all these words and pondered them in her heart. The shepherds returned, glorifying and praising God for all they had heard and seen, as it had been told them.

LUKE 2:8–20

Liturgical dance has made its way into some churches. However, Christians on the whole have not been enthusiastic about linking dance with religion, and the image of dance is strangely underused. But what a wonderful idea it conveys—the whole universe filled with the strains of divine love, all heaven moving in harmony to this music and we called also to hear and let our lives flow in grace.

Our eyes are drawn to the angels dancing in the sky below the great luminous circle. Holding hands, with flowers dropping between them, they flow and fly with graceful joy. There are twelve of them—twelve being a highly significant number in the New Testament. Below these are three angels kneeling on the roof of the stable, again in a small circle. Then at the bottom of the picture three angels embrace human beings in gestures which themselves seem part of the dance.

Sandro Botticelli (1447–1515) in the early part of his career painted some mythological paintings, amongst them his famous *Primavera* (Spring) and *The Birth of Venus*. There is evidence that his patron at this time had strong interests in Platonic philosophy interpreted in a particular way, so that these apparently secular pictures had a deep moral or metaphysical significance. Later, Botticelli's art became increasingly ecstatic and intense, *The Mystic Nativity* coming from this period. It reacted against the naturalism of the early Renaissance and revived certain elements of an earlier style, a delicate sentiment, a feminine grace and an emphasis on the evocative capabilities of line. It is in this last quality that Botticelli's art is so outstanding and so well suited to conveying the idea of the heavenly dance.

At the birth of God's Son heaven and earth danced. For heaven and earth embrace. All things are filled with divine music and we too are invited to move our lives with grace, in harmony with divine love.

NATIVITY by Piero della Francesca

We do not have many surviving paintings by Piero della Francesca (1415–75) but each one has a striking quality that has particularly appealed to twentieth-century art lovers. For me it has to do with his clear line and sense of light and spaciousness.

In this painting, the eye can be drawn by some fascinating details, such as the miniature Florence in the background on the right as we look at the painting, with windows and lanes shown; the Tuscan landscape in the distance on the left; the odd figure of Joseph sitting on a saddle turned away from the main scene and the grass growing in the roof of the run-down stable. Some of these details reflect the influence of northern tradition, such as the child lying on the ground and the realism of the animals. But, however one's eye may roam around, it is drawn back time and again to the joyous group of musician angels. Whether playing a lute or singing they are totally absorbed in the business of making music in honour of the Christ child. There is another group of singers in Florence, carved by Luca della Robbia which show the same utter absorption in music and which may have influenced Piero. In both we see the singers with their mouths open and can almost hear the notes coming out.

Behind the singers a donkey is braying. This detail is unusual though there are some other examples from northern Italy and it is also known from French books of hours. The braying donkey and the singing angels stand in creative juxtaposition. Both, in their different ways, are praising their creator. The donkey does it simply by giving voice. The musicians do it in trained, disciplined harmony, utilizing both voice and instrument. Human beings bring all their skills to bear—the whole tradition of art—in the service of the Saviour.

So it is above all praise, sheer joy, that this Nativity conveys. Much of our life is a hurrying on to something else, doing something in order that a goal might be achieved. But joy is an end in itself: joy in life, in the Saviour, in God as God.

This painting brings to mind George Herbert, who also loved music and studded his poetry with musical images. That poetry too expresses a channelled, disciplined joy. This is a joy in which all creation is invited to share— the ass by braying, the angels in their ceaseless praise and we human beings, rejoicing in the gift of life which God has bestowed upon us, in the gift of Christ who comes to redeem our warped world, in God as God for his own sake.

Let all the world in ev'ry corner sing
My God and King.
GEORGE HERBERT

THE NATIVITY, AT NIGHT by Geertgen tot Sint Jans

I fell in love with the Geertgen *Nativity* nearly twenty years ago and its gentle stillness moves me still. The first impression is of light: light glowing from the Christ child, lighting up the faces of Mary and the angels as they gaze down at the crib, lighting up the angel against the dark sky. The darkness is really black, the black of night and the black of a world in the grip of evil. But the light of Christ illuminates our night.

Looming out of the darkness are the two huge faces of the ox and the ass, which have been part of Nativity scenes from the earliest icons. Their presence is due to Isaiah 1:3, which Christians quickly applied to this scene. In contrast to humanity which does not know, does not understand, 'The ox knows its owner, and the ass its master's crib.'

At the top left-hand side of the painting can be discerned the shepherds, an unusual, realistic view, rather like an aerial photograph. At the right-hand side is Joseph, with a look of guileless goodness on his face.

It is this quality of tender, innocent goodness that above all pervades this scene. We see it in the faces of the angels but above all in Mary. Mary is looking at the child as a mother might bend over her babe in pram or bed, with wonder and love. Yet in Mary's look there is also a sense of more than ordinary wonder, more than ordinary adoration, at the birth of the Son of God. There is nothing strident or attention-seeking here. Just a gentle love. There is a solemn reverence in the faces of the angels too, which are childlike, for it is necessary to become in one sense like a child in order to see the kingdom of God.

Geertgen painted his *Nativity* in Haarlem about 1490. He was a lay brother in the religious order of St John, and known as Gerard. For me there is a connection between his humble, self-effacing role as a lay brother and the quality of gentle innocence that suffuses this painting: its quiet, tender, attentiveness.

Our eyes focus first on the dark cavernous stable. This is no pretty byre but a working stable with ropes hanging down and a ladder propped against the side. But the darkness seems to reflect and take on the character of the mysterious vastness of the universe outside. Small and lonely we huddle together for comfort.

So our eyes are drawn to the little group gathered round the light, close to the light and close to one another. From the light of the Christ child we receive light; it is reflected on our faces and, shining on the beams and struts of the stable, it sends soft gleams into our darkness.

For most of Christian history the human imagination has been stirred first and foremost by the kings. It was only in the fifteenth and sixteenth centuries that the shepherds began to be represented in their own right. They are part of a scene which finds its wonderful high-point in this Rembrandt.

For the first part of his artistic life Rembrandt (1606–69) painted in a grandiose, baroque manner. Then in the early 1640s when he began to run into troubles, including the deaths of three children in infancy and his wife

Saskia, he dramatically changed his approach. He focused on the human, the ordinary. In this scene there are no angels, no heavenly music. The faces are such as Rembrandt would have found anywhere, yet full of such dignity and sweetness. To the edge of the picture on the right two of the shepherds turn to each other to talk, whilst below them a little boy kneels holding his dog. To the left of the picture some cows go their own way. Rembrandt did not depict the traditional ox and ass, based upon Isaiah 1:3, but animals that would normally be found in a stable. Close to the light Joseph bends over, proud, pondering, like any father not quite knowing what to say. Mary and two shepherds kneel in awe and tenderness.

Here heaven is revealed in ordinary people, through ordinary things. It makes us look at the ordinary in a new way. For if heaven is in this scene in a special way, heaven is in every scene in some way. The ordinary, familiar faces and people of our daily round are also touched by the dignity, grace and tenderness of the incarnate God.

*A*fter eight days had passed, it was time to circumcise the child; and he was called Jesus, the name given by the angel before he was conceived in the womb.

When the time came for their purification according to the law of Moses, they brought him up to Jerusalem to present him to the Lord (as it is written in the law of the Lord, 'Every firstborn male shall be designated as holy to the Lord'), and they offered a sacrifice according to what is stated in the law of the Lord, 'a pair of turtle-doves or two young pigeons.'

Now there was a man in Jerusalem whose name was Simeon; this man was righteous and devout, looking forward to the consolation of Israel, and the Holy Spirit rested on him. It had been revealed to him by the Holy Spirit that he would not see death before he had seen the Lord's Messiah. Guided by the Spirit, Simeon came into the temple; and when the parents brought in the child Jesus, to do for him what was customary under the law, Simeon took him in his arms and praised God, saying,

'Master, now you are dismissing your servant in peace,
according to your word;
for my eyes have seen your salvation,
which you have prepared in the presence of all peoples,
a light for revelation to the Gentiles
and for glory to your people Israel.'

And the child's father and mother were amazed at what was being said about him. Then Simeon blessed them and said to his mother Mary, 'This child is destined for the falling and the rising of many in Israel, and to be a sign that will be opposed so that the inner thoughts of many will be revealed—and a sword will pierce your own soul too.'

There was also a prophet Anna the daughter of Phanuel, of the tribe of Asher. She was of a great age, having lived with her husband seven years after her marriage, then as a widow to the age of eighty-four. She never left the temple but worshipped there with fasting and prayer night and day. At that moment she came, and began to praise God and to speak about the child to all who were looking for the redemption of Jerusalem.

LUKE 2:21–38

THE PRESENTATION OF CHRIST IN THE TEMPLE

This feast has been known by different names. Sometimes it is called the Purification of the Blessed Virgin Mary; hence it takes place on 2 February, forty days after Christmas. It is also described as Candlemas, because candles are used in the liturgy to symbolize a light to lighten the Gentiles. It is also called 'Meeting' (*Hypapante*) in the Orthodox Church, because it is a meeting of Simeon, representing devout people of old, with the long-expected Saviour.

Works of Christian art that can easily be overlooked are the reliefs, usually on the panels of the doors of cathedrals or churches, in wood or metal. Many of these, which often set out to show the whole Christian story in detail, are delightful. The thirteenth-century panel from Pisa Cathedral shown here pictures Anna with raised hands giving thanks behind Simeon. Mary is presenting Jesus, while Joseph follows behind with the gifts. The inscription reads, 'Simeon receives the boy'.

THE SONG OF SIMEON by Rembrandt

Rembrandt loved this scene and painted different aspects of it over the years. Here he concentrates exclusively on the face of Simeon and the young child. Interestingly, this focus was also a development in the art of the Orthodox Church, with Simeon shown holding the child rather like Mary in the Icon of Loving Kindness.

This painting has been badly damaged and it is likely that the figure of Mary in the background was not painted by Rembrandt himself. It was Rembrandt's last painting and it lay in his house unfinished after his death in 1669.

The face of Simeon in the painting seems perfectly to convey the feeling of his song, 'Lord now lettest thou thy servant depart in peace, according to thy word: for mine eyes have seen thy salvation.' Simeon, with his eyes half closed and his mouth open, is lost in prayer to the God who is close to him. He holds the child gently and reverentially but his being seems already half withdrawn from this world to be for ever with God.

A nd having been warned in a dream not to return to Herod, they left for
their own country by another road.

MATTHEW 2:12

AN ANGEL APPEARS TO THE THREE KINGS IN A DREAM by Gislebertus

This charming carving appears on a capital in Autun Cathedral, in the centre of France. It was carved by a man named Gislebertus, the greatest sculptor of his period and one of the few whose name we know. We know his name because on one of his carvings he put the words *'Gislebertus hoc fecit'*—'Gislebertus made this'—a sign of the great esteem in which he was held by his contemporaries. He carried out the work in Autun between 1125 and 1135.

Many people today have come to appreciate the art of this, Romanesque, period because of its expressive nature and stylized form. One of the advantages of modern art is that it has enabled us to appreciate this kind of art more than our predecessors, who tended to prefer art that was either more naturalistic or classical.

Gislebertus carved four scenes from Matthew's Gospel on the capitals at Autun: the Wise Men before Herod, the Adoration of the Wise Men, the Dream of the Wise Men, shown here, and the Flight into Egypt. Here he adopts a Romanesque convention of showing the three kings in bed together under the one blanket. It must have been uncomfortable in the bed, wearing their crowns, but this was of course the only way of indicating that they really were kings. The embroidered blanket seems to move in harmony with the face, halo, sleeves and wing of the angel in one graceful, circular movement. It is as though the angel has slipped suddenly and silently in. With one hand he points to the star which will guide them safely home. With the other he touches one of the kings, who opens his eyes. The angel, despite his broken nose, still conveys a wonderful sense of gentleness.

This carving, like the story on which it is based, wanted to convey two truths. First, God cares for each one of us. Having guided the three kings to the Christ child, he did not then abandon them. On the contrary, they are to be seen safely home, away from the angry plotting of Herod. Secondly, in caring for us, God guides us. This is symbolized by a star in the heavens. But for us it may be a light within. People in the ancient world had no problem about believing that God, through his angels, spoke to us in dreams. During the twentieth century we have rediscovered the importance of dreams in showing us more about ourselves. Moreover, as the Holy Spirit works through the whole of us, he works also through our unconscious, including our dreams. In understanding our dreams we may be able to understand more about ourselves and therefore more about the direction in which our lives should go. But God guides us in many different ways, not just through dreams.

What Gislebertus conveys so beautifully is the gentle touch of the angel. The flight barely disturbs the air. Suddenly he is there, a sweet and silent presence. The guidance of God is rarely loud and overwhelming. It is usually the slightest touch, the nudge, the hint.

Now after they had left, an angel of the Lord appeared to Joseph in a dream and said, 'Get up, take the child and his mother, and flee to Egypt, and remain there until I tell you; for Herod is about to search for the child, to destroy him.' Then Joseph got up, took the child and his mother by night, and went to Egypt, and remained there until the death of Herod. This was to fulfil what had been spoken by the Lord through the prophet, 'Out of Egypt I have called my son.'

MATTHEW 2:13–15

Egypt had very special associations for the first Christians. It was the country to which the patriarch Joseph went to escape famine. It was the place where the infant Moses was saved from the slaughter of infants by a murderous Pharoah. It was the country from which God delivered the people of Israel in a great exodus. All these themes are echoed in the story of the flight of the Holy Family to Egypt and their safe return after Herod's death. A new Joseph, the husband of Mary, goes down to Egypt. The infant Jesus escapes the murderous machinations of King Herod, much as Moses had done. Now all humanity is to be delivered from bondage in a new exodus focused in Jesus. For Matthew this is all contained in the text, 'Out of Egypt I called my son', which is a quotation of Hosea 11:1, with a reference to Exodus 4:22, where the people of Israel as a whole is called God's first-born son. The people of Israel were set in a relationship of sonship to God. This relationship is summed up in Jesus. He lives out the vocation of the whole people for us all.

The biblical story is told without detail. However, early Christian writers elaborated with many fanciful legends. Not surprisingly a number of places in Egypt claim to be where the Holy Family stopped or stayed, especially the Church of Abur Serghis (Sargah) in Old Cairo. Coptic Christians in Egypt trace their descent to the earliest Christian mission in Alexandria founded, according to tradition, by Mark; today they may number as many as ten million. A church of great faith which has survived in a Muslim country for more than a thousand years, it has a profound spirituality based on its monasteries. Understandably they particularly prize the connection between themselves and the flight of the Holy Family to Egypt for refuge.

In depictions of this scene from the fourth to the sixth century, the arrival of the Holy Family in Egypt was sometimes cast in a form of an entry by the emperor, an *adventus*. A youth or an angel leads the donkey on which Mary sits holding the Christ child, with Joseph following. Sometimes Egypt is personified. The sixth-century book, known as the *Gospel of Pseudo Matthew*, recounts some fabulous tales of Christ's infancy, including incidents from the Flight into Egypt. The Holy Family rested under a palm tree, which bent down to feed the hungry Mary. When they came into an Egyptian city, Heliopolis, which was full of idols, the idols fell, shattered. Later depictions of the scene, however, tended to emphasize the humanity of the characters. Joseph was depicted leading the donkey, sometimes looking straight ahead, as in the sculptures by Gislebertus at Autun, later looking back protectively at Mary. In mosaics at Palermo in Sicily, Joseph is shown with the Christ child on his back.

Christ the Son of God and the Holy Family become refugees, of whom, sadly, there are many millions in the world today. But Jesus is not simply a victim. In this icon he is shown on the donkey blessing the onlooker, whom both he and Mary face. Even in his identification with human flight and suffering he blesses us. Above all he blesses us by taking us into his own Sonship. 'Out of Egypt I called my son' applies not only to the people of Israel as a whole, not only to Jesus but, through him, to us also. For we have been delivered from bondage to sin, from the tyranny of death, and have entered, as St Paul says, into the glorious liberty of the children of God. As God's sons and daughters we have access to him.

THE REST ON THE FLIGHT INTO EGYPT by Orazio Gentileschi

Late medieval artists liked to depict all sorts of episodes from the Flight into Egypt of which there is no mention in Matthew's Gospel. Some of them are derived from the infancy stories in the sixth-century *Gospel of Pseudo Matthew*, and others from elaborations of this in popular literature. Scenes of the Rest on the Flight into Egypt were very popular, particularly in Dutch art and, in the sixteenth and seventeenth centuries, overtook pictures of the Flight into Egypt in general popularity. No doubt this was partly because it provided artists like Claude an opportunity to paint evocative landscapes. But it also enabled them to draw out the human features of the story—the exhaustion of the Holy Family, and the care of Joseph for Mary and the Christ child. Rembrandt depicted this scene a number of times. Particularly in his painting of it in the National Gallery of Ireland, he conveys a sense of the vulnerability of the little group, set in a large landscape and sky. Joseph, Mary and the child are huddled together round a fire under some trees—like so many refugee families feeling that they only have one another in a hostile world.

Gentileschi (1563–1647) was an Italian painter much influenced by Caravaggio. He developed a style which was toned-down from that of Caravaggio, as in this picture, using few figures clearly disposed and painted in cool colours with sharp outlines. The use of light is also reminscent of Caravaggio. Gentileschi worked in England at the court of Charles I, where he was much honoured. There are a number of his paintings in Britain, including this one in the City Museum and Art Gallery, Birmingham.

It is a striking, even haunting scene, which could be a still from a film by one of our better continental film producers. It has a slightly surreal, modern atmosphere, achieved by the broad expanse of unusual colours, the clear outline and, above all, the light.

Our eye is drawn first to the head of the donkey, looming up behind the wall. It is much larger than a normal perspective would depict it—although behind the wall, the length of the head is almost the length of Mary's sitting body. It is this head set against the grey and light of the sky which gives the painting its mysterious quality. What is the donkey thinking? We are brought up against the mystery of animal life and so against the mystery of existence itself. The donkey which bowed its head over the crib, which later was to carry Christ into Jerusalem, here stands silent as the Holy Family rest.

Joseph is spread-eagled, certainly dozing if not fully asleep, utterly exhausted. The donkey can rest, Joseph can rest, but Mary, like so many mothers, has work to do—she feeds the infant child from her breast. If we were pernickety, we might suggest that the child looks more like a two-year-old, just beginning to walk, rather than a babe in arms. But Gentileschi wanted to show to the full this human, sensuous scene.

The cool colours, the unearthly light, the brooding head of the donkey—all combine to evoke a sense of the vividness and mystery of existence. This is a human scene—a child at the breast, a man exhausted; but it is not ordinary, for nothing is ordinary. Here we sense the sheer shock of being.

When Herod saw that he had been tricked by the wise men, he was infuriated, and he sent and killed all the children in and around Bethlehem who were two years old or under, according to the time that he had learned from the wise men. Then was fulfilled what had been spoken through the prophet Jeremiah:

A voice was heard in Ramah,
wailing and loud lamentation,
Rachel weeping for her children;
she refused to be consoled,
because they are no more.'

MATTHEW 2:16–18

MASSACRE OF THE INNOCENTS by Giotto

This scene begins to appear in Christian art from the fifth century. By the sixteenth century it had become a favourite theme for artists who wished to show their skill in depicting violence. It is not difficult to see why. Sadly, we human beings not only inflict suffering on our fellow human beings, we sometimes revel in depicting or watching it, as, for example, on the cinema screen or in 'video nasties'. Yet, there is a great deal of violence in the world and we have to face this. It is a terrible shock after the joy of Christmas, to come on 28 December to the story of Herod's massacre of the children, but no doubt it is salutary. For, tragically, this is still so much part of the world in which we live.

In this fresco by Giotto, part of his miraculous series in the Scrovegni Chapel in Padua, the artist does not revel in the violence. Nevertheless, it is shocking enough. You can feel the anguish of the mothers, as their babes are snatched away. You almost shudder before the soldier about to spike another child with his sword. The growing pile of babies, heaped one on top of the other moves us to pity. Yet those babes seem almost peacefully asleep.

For the church has never seen these innocents simply as victims. They have also been regarded in some sense as martyrs, those who died for the faith even though they were not old enough to make a conscious decision to do so. In the words of the seventeenth-century Anglican writer, Jeremy Taylor, these children 'were so soon made stars, when they shined in their little orbs and participations of eternity'.

These innocents stand for all those whose innocence is violated, all those children cruelly treated, victims of direct malevolence or suffering brought about by political injustice. The Nativity story is beautiful and it has been made especially beautiful in music and poetry and art. This beauty cannot be an escape from the brutal reality of the world. Nevertheless, in the light of the resurrection of Christ, we have the hope that the beauty of God will win through and that innocence is not lost for ever. Rather, it is to be taken up, transfigured, to become luminous with the light of Christ himself.

The Christ child for us today

NATIVITY WITH BURNING BUSH by Albert Herbert

Our eye is drawn first by the figure of Mary, a figure of transparent innocence and goodness. She holds the Christ child, offering him to the world, and her whole being is poised in this gesture of offering.

The man kneeling is an old man, one who has made not just a physical journey but a spiritual one, and his face reflects the wisdom acquired. He kneels and adores. But, above all, his hands and arms are outstretched to receive. It is as though he is kneeling to receive Holy Communion. His body, reflecting his heart, is open to welcome the incarnate God.

These figures are set against a dark hill looming in the background, the skyline opening up to light. The darkness of the hill is not, however, sombre or threatening. It is the darkness of God himself, the 'cloud of unknowing' in which the Nativity is set.

God is not only a dazzling darkness but a burning bush. To the right of the picture is the burning bush in which God appeared to Moses. One traditional icon depicts Mary in the burning bush. Here she is not in the bush but, as it were, having just stepped from it. The Christ child comes from the mystery of the Godhead, at once dazzling darkness and fiery glory.

At the bottom right-hand corner is a patch of light. A spot of light on the carpet, a sudden shaft of sunlight through the curtain, can lift our spirits. This is the light of the Spirit who lights us on our way, a friendly, accessible spot of light.

Albert Herbert was born in 1925. He received no religious education and for many years had no interest in religion, but in 1958 at the age of 33 he was received into the Roman Catholic Church. His painting has gone through a number of different phases but in recent years he has had his sympathy for Christian symbolism re-awakened. He has been regarded as the most significant religious painter to emerge in England in the 1980s and is much admired by many discerning critics. He is not interested in depicting the historical accuracy of the biblical stories but in exploring their symbolic significance. His pictures, with their childlike images, have a disarming simplicity and directness. They have a meaning which goes deeper than the conscious mind, touching our spirit in ways that we may not always be able to fathom or describe.

In this picture we kneel with the wise one to receive Christ into our heart, the Christ who comes to us from the unfathomable darkness and glory of God and who, through his Spirit, lights us on our way.

NATIVITY SCENE 1990 by Beryl Cook

Beryl Cook (born 1926) has been described as Britain's most popular painter. Perhaps this is because so many people identify with her large, cheerful, self-confident women. The Madonna in this scene is very far from the traditional image of a slight young girl. She is large and in her thirties. But clearly she is in no way got down by this. For her, 'fat is beautiful'. She is a woman with a very proper sense of her own value. She is a woman who will hold things together when everyone else has collapsed. She will be at the centre encouraging and cheering people up when everyone else is depressed. She is the one upon whom others depend, who won't let them down, who presses on despite all difficulties.

She has also imparted some of her own sense of self-worth to her child. He is no less exuberant and confident (a bit overweight too). He reaches out ready to clap his hands in response to the angels flying around him. When bright objects are dangled over babies in prams their eyes are caught up and they delight. So here the Christ child is fascinated by the angels with whom he wants to play.

The whole picture has something of the air of a child's farm set, the ass and ox on one side, the lambs on the other and the light lifting above the fields and glistening on the leaves of the tree. Lambs are traditionally symbols of the Passion but here it is their innocence and curiosity that are to the fore. Wordsworth said that 'heaven lies about us in our infancy'. Thomas Traherne had the same heightened awareness of childhood as a time of angelic wonder. The same sense is conveyed by this painting.

Beryl Cook does not usually paint Christian themes. But I am glad she has depicted the Nativity. We can look at this picture and feel that the world is a better place than we imagined. Children are yet born into it with a sense of wonder and delight. Mothers in all shapes and sizes enjoy being themselves and convey that sense of enjoyment to their children. For life, and the good things of life, we praise you, O God.

THE NATIVITY STAINED GLASS WINDOW by John Piper,

Modern Christianity has sometimes been criticized for having too low a view of nature and animals. This was certainly not true of the Middle Ages. Then there was a legend that all animals become articulate on Christmas Day and there was a special mass in which the choristers took the parts of various animals and birds. This legend goes back at least to the fourth-century hymn writer, Prudentius, who wrote a poem on the subject. In some of the rural districts of Brittany and Gascony it is apparently still performed. A sheet of carols published in 1701 has a picture of mother and child in the stable surrounded by animals making their characteristic sound. Down the side is the explanation:

The cock croweth: 'Christus natus est (Christ is born).'
The raven asked: 'Quando? (when?)'
The crow replied: 'Hoc nocte (this night).'
The ox cried out: 'Ubi? Id Ubi? (where, where?)'
The sheep bleated out: 'Bethlem! Bethlem!'
A voice from heaven sounded: 'Gloria in Excelsis (Glory be on high).'
Whilst armies of angels sang: 'Alleluia!
Salutation and glory and honour and power be to the Lord our God!'

This theme was repeated in French, Italian and Portugese poems. The scene is shown in a wall painting at Shuldred Priory and it is the subject of Charles Causley's 'The Animals' Carol'. This begins:

Christus natus est! The cock
Carols on the morning dark.
Quando? croaks the raven stiff
Freezing on the broken cliff.
Hoc nocte, replies the crow
Beating high above the snow.
Ubi? Ubi? booms the ox
From its cavern in the rocks.
Bethlehem, then bleats the sheep
Huddled on the winter steep . . .

John Piper has portrayed this theme in vivid colours in one of his stained-glass windows due to be placed in St Mary's, Iffley. The tree shoots up to the sky, full of life and strength. We remember all those references in the Bible to the Tree of Life. In the branches of the tree rest various animals—the cock, a goose, a raven or crow and an owl. At the bottom a sheep bleats 'Bethlem! Bethlem!'

Behind the tree, the sky is getting light. Dark surrounds the window with a lighter blue towards the centre and white behind the cock. The night of sin flees away as the light of Christ dawns on the world. At this dawn the whole of the animal world joins in praise.

Human beings are indeed the crown of God's creation, for we are capable of rational speech and love and prayer. But we are not isolated from the animal world. They too in their own way reflect God's glory. They too in their own way offer praise. We join with them in singing *Gloria in Excelsis!*

Christus natus est!

Quando? quando?

in hac nocte...

Ubi? ubi?

Bethlem! Bethlem!

Acknowledgments

We acknowledge the following for permission to use the photographs on the pages stated:

Title page: As page 53.

Page 11: Icon is from the Byzantine Museum of Paphos and property of the Holy See of Paphos.

Page 13: Photo Vatican Museums.

Page 14: Photo Vatican Museums.

Page 15: Hirmer fotoarchiv, Munich. Ampulla from the treasury of Monza Cathedral.

Page 17: Reproduced by courtesy of the Director and University Librarian, the John Rylands University Library of Manchester.

Page 21: Photo: Scala, Florence.

Page 25: Courtesy of the Fogg Art Museum, Harvard University Museums.

Page 27: Photo by permission of Hermann Schulz.

Page 31: SCR Photo Library.

Page 32: SCR Photo Library.

Page 33: Icon is from the Byzantine Museum of Paphos and property of the Holy See of Paphos.

Page 34: SCR Photo Library.

Page 35: SCR Photo Library.

Page 36: Editions Houvet, Chartres.

Page 37: Sonia Halliday Photographs.

Page 39: *A Multitude of the Heavenly Host* by Japanese artist Yasuo Ueno, taken from the book *The Bible Through Asian Eyes*. By permission of the Asian Christian Art Association.

Page 41: Editions 'Hannibal', Athens.

Page 43: Published by permission of the Director of Antiquities and the Cyprus Museum.

Page 47: Associated University Presses.

Page 49: Photo: Scala, Florence.

Page 51: Photo: Scala, Florence.

Page 53: J. Paul Getty Museum, Malibu, California/Bridgeman Art Library.

Page 55: Castle Museum Norwich.

Page 59: Reproduced by courtesy of the Trustees, The National Gallery, London.

Page 61: Reproduced by courtesy of the Trustees, The National Gallery, London.

Page 63: Reproduced by courtesy of the Trustees, The National Gallery, London.

Page 65: Reproduced by courtesy of the Trustees, The National Gallery, London.

Page 69: Richard Harries.

Page 71: Photo: Nationalmuseum, SKM, Stockholm.

Page 75: Abbé Denis Grivot.

Page 79: Icon from the Coptic Museum (Mathaf Al-Qibti), Old Cairo.

Page 81: Birmingham City Museum and Art Galleries/Bridgeman Art Library.

Page 85: Photo: Scala, Florence.

Page 87: Private collection, courtesy of England & Co Gallery, London.

Page 89: Beryl Cook, *Nativity Scene 1990*, first published in *Bouncers* by Beryl Cook © 1991. Published by Victor Gollancz. Reproduced by arrangement with Rogers, Coleridge & White Ltd.

Page 91: *The Nativity* by John Piper. Reproduced by permission of Mrs Myfanwy Piper.

The poem 'The Animals' Carol' on page 90 copyright © Charles Causley, reprinted by permission of David Higham Associates.